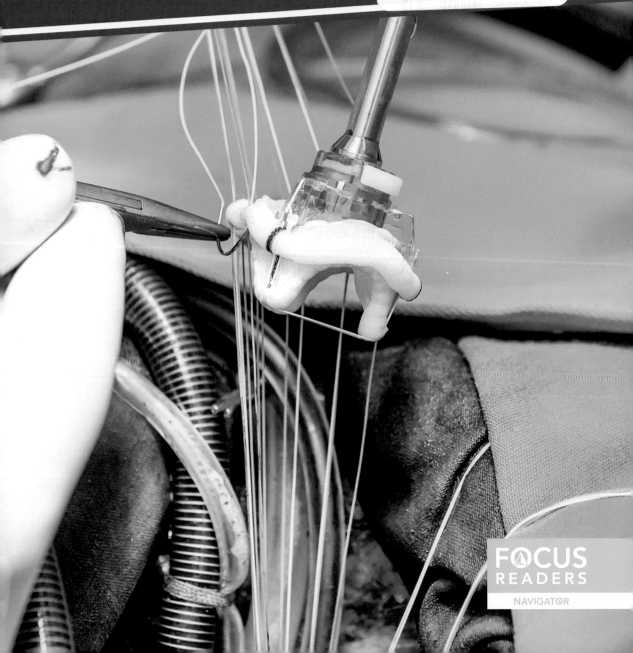

ENGINEERING THE HUMAN BODY

ARTIFICIAL ORGANS

Gagne

D0121068

FOCUS
READERS

NAVIGATOR

WWW.FOCUSREADERS.COM

Focus Readers is distributed by North Star Editions:
sales@northstareditions.com | 888-417-0195

Produced for Focus Readers by Red Line Editorial.

Content Consultant: Keith E. Cook, Professor of Biomedical Engineering, Carnegie Mellon University

Photographs ©: pirke/Shutterstock Images, cover, 1; Rick Bowmer/AP Images, 4–5; Courtesy of syncardia.com, 7; kalewa/Shutterstock Images, 9, 10–11; StanislauV/Shutterstock Images, 13; Aleksandr Ivasenko/Shutterstock Images, 15; Dee Breger/Science Source, 17; Michael Holahan/AP Images, 18–19; Bangkoker/Shutterstock Images, 21; BSIP/Newscom, 23; Philippe Psaila/Science Source, 24–25; Natalia Sinjushina & Evgeniy Meyke/Shutterstock Images, 27; Maurice Savage/Alamy, 29

Library of Congress Cataloging-in-Publication Data
Names: Gagne, Tammy, author.
Title: Artificial organs / by Tammy Gagne.
Description: Lake Elmo, MN : Focus Readers, 2020. | Series: Engineering the
  human body | Audience: Grades 4 to 6. | Includes bibliographical
  references and index.
Identifiers: LCCN 2018053926 (print) | LCCN 2018060831 (ebook) | ISBN
  9781641859691 (pdf) | ISBN 9781641859004 (e-book) | ISBN 9781641857628
  (hardcover) | ISBN 9781641858311 (pbk.)
Subjects: LCSH: Artificial organs--Juvenile literature. | Medical
  innovations--Juvenile literature.
Classification: LCC RD130 (ebook) | LCC RD130 .G34 2020 (print) | DDC
  617.956--dc23
LC record available at https://lccn.loc.gov/2018053926

Printed in the United States of America
Mankato, MN
May, 2019

ABOUT THE AUTHOR

Tammy Gagne has written more than 200 books for both adults and children. She resides in northern New England with her husband and son. Her most recent titles include *Exoskeletons* and *Extra Senses*.

TABLE OF CONTENTS

Akutsu-III Total Artificial Heart c. 1981

CHAPTER 1

LIFE-SAVING SURGERY

In 2018, 10-year-old Gabriel Gonzalez collapsed. His condition was serious. His heart had stopped working properly. Doctors could not fix Gabriel's heart. He needed a new one. The surgery to give a patient a new organ is called a transplant. Without this surgery, Gabriel would die. But no hearts were available at that time.

A doctor holds up a total artificial heart, similar to the one implanted in Gabriel Gonzalez.

To save his life, doctors gave Gabriel an artificial heart. The device kept him alive while he waited for a **donor**. Months later, Gabriel received the needed heart transplant.

The heart is an organ in the human body. Organs are sets of tissues that have specific jobs. For example, the heart pumps blood throughout the body. Some organs, called vital organs, keep people alive. These organs include the heart, liver, kidneys, and lungs. Other organs help people interact with the world. These organs include the eyes and ears.

Doctors try to fix an organ when it stops working. Sometimes, organs cannot be fixed. An organ transplant becomes necessary. Healthy people can choose to donate their organs after their deaths.

ARTIFICIAL VS. NATURAL

At first glance, an artificial heart might not look like a natural one. But its parts have similar functions. What matters most is how the organ works.

ARTIFICIAL HEART

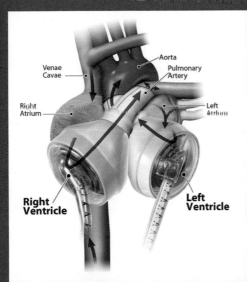

Venae Cavae

Aorta

Pulmonary Artery

Right Atrium

Left Atrium

Right Ventricle

Left Ventricle

NATURAL HEART

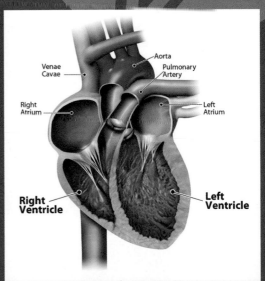

Venae Cavae

Aorta

Pulmonary Artery

Right Atrium

Left Atrium

Right Ventricle

Left Ventricle

People can donate certain organs, such as the kidney, while they are alive. But there are not enough donors.

Technology offers another option. Patients can receive artificial organs. These devices take the place of unhealthy organs. They perform the same jobs as natural organs. They can save patients

ARTIFICIAL EYES

A **bionic** eye can help people with vision loss. Doctors place this device near or inside one eye. The device sends messages from the eye to the brain. The result is a visual image. A bionic eye is not as effective as natural sight. But it allows people to identify basic objects.

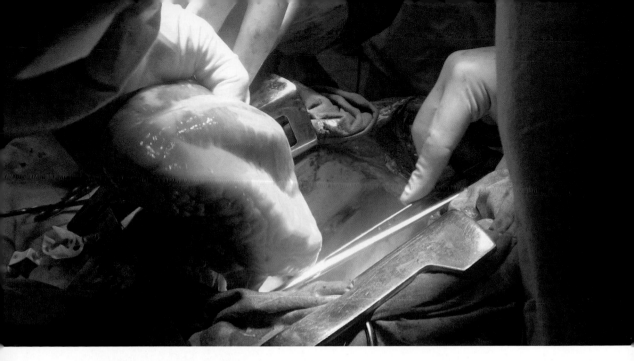

People can decide if they want to donate their organs. Doctors harvest healthy organs after the donor's death.

who would die without donor organs. Artificial organs are human-made. As a result, more of them are available.

Scientists have designed many different artificial organs. Some are still being researched. They must pass a strict testing process. Then they can be used to help patients.

CHAPTER 2

ADDRESSING A NEED

The average wait for a heart transplant in the United States is six months. Some patients die while waiting. Others don't even make the waiting list because of the shortage of organs. A donor organ must pass certain tests to be selected for transplant. Matching available organs with patients can be difficult.

Doctors prepare a human heart for transplant.

Organ transplants pose additional challenges. Some patients get sicker after a transplant. The **immune system** can sense something different in the body. It attacks the new organ. Medicine can help prevent this problem. But sometimes a patient's body still rejects the new organ. The body reacts differently with artificial organs. These organs do not bring new human tissue into the body. The immune system cannot destroy an artificial organ.

The first devices made to help failing organs worked outside patients' bodies. Willem Kolff invented the first artificial kidney machine in 1943. Kidneys remove

Patients with a donor organ take daily medicine. The pills keep the immune system from attacking the transplant.

toxins from the blood. Kolff's machine could do the same thing. He used it on patients with failing kidneys. His first patients did not survive. Then one patient recovered the use of her kidneys after being treated. She lived for another seven years. Kolff's device eventually led to today's **dialysis** machines.

Kolff also worked on the first artificial organ. Artificial organs work from inside a patient's body. In 1982, Kolff and Robert Jarvik invented the first artificial heart used for long periods in humans. Biomedical engineers have improved this device. The first patient to receive the

BIOMEDICAL ENGINEERS

Biomedical engineers have both medical and engineering knowledge. They understand the human body. They also know how to design and build tools. Some of them design artificial organs. Others make tools for doctors. These tools tell doctors what is wrong in their patients' bodies. Many medical advances come from biomedical engineers.

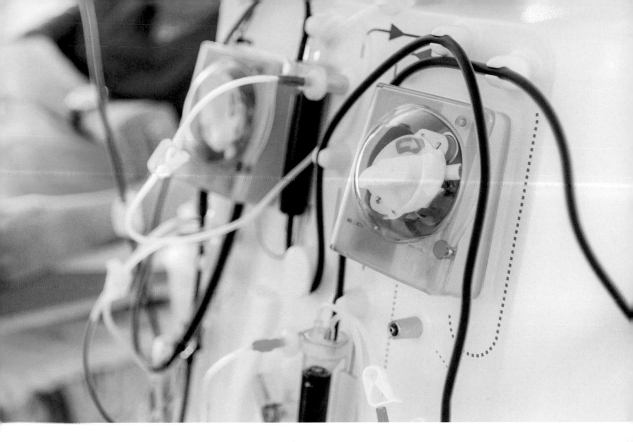

A dialysis machine draws blood out of a patient's body, filters the blood, and returns the blood to the body.

heart lived 112 days. Today, patients can live for years with an artificial heart.

Artificial organs are often temporary. Artificial hearts still do not last as long as natural ones. But they keep patients alive until donor organs are available.

ARTIFICIAL LUNGS

The lungs are vital organs. They take in the oxygen needed for human life. Humans breathe in air. The lungs take oxygen from the air. The oxygen goes into the blood. The lungs also remove carbon dioxide from the blood. Humans breathe out the carbon dioxide.

Sometimes the lungs stop working properly. Scientists have created an artificial lung. It is a box with two tubes coming out of it. Inside the box are fabrics made of tiny threads. Oxygen from an oxygen tank flows through the threads.

The box is strapped to the patient's chest. The tubes connect to two of the patient's **arteries**. The patient's heart pumps blood through one of the tubes. The blood enters the box. It flows by the fabrics. Oxygen from the threads enters the blood. Carbon dioxide from the blood enters the

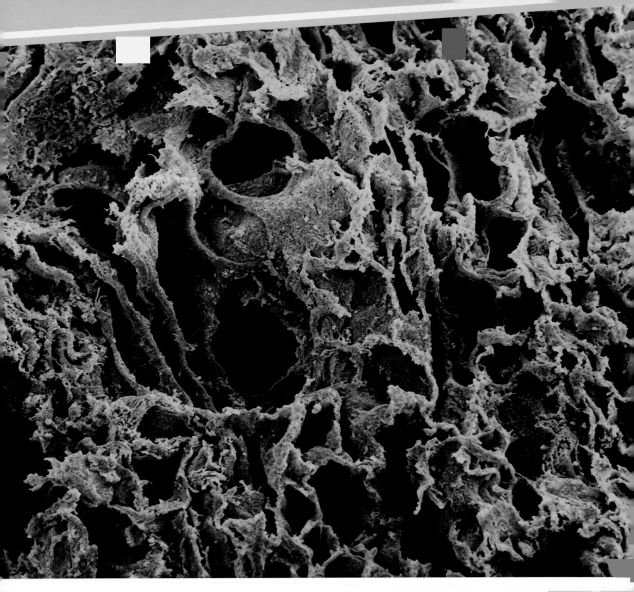

These tiny air sacs are found in natural lungs. Artificial lungs use tiny threads instead.

threads. It is released from the blood. Then, the blood leaves the box through the second tube. The blood brings oxygen to the rest of the body.

CHAPTER 3

TECHNOLOGY TODAY

Technology in biomedical engineering has come a long way. Scientists can now make certain parts of organs from human cells. In Sweden, a patient had a tumor growing on his trachea. This tube carries air from the mouth to the lungs. The patient needed a new one. In 2011, he received the first artificial trachea.

Scientists can grow human skin. They mix healthy skin cells with the nutrients cells need to multiply.

Doctors used a plastic tube as a frame. First, they placed **stem cells** from the patient's body over the tube. Next, they removed his trachea. Then, they replaced it with the tube. The stem cells grew into the surrounding tissue. The cells kept growing inside the patient's body. In doing so, they connected the tube to the body's natural tissue. The stem cells made the body less likely to reject the new organ. The patient lived with the artificial trachea for more than a year.

Some artificial organs are especially hard to make. The skin is the human body's largest organ. Among other jobs, it plays a crucial role in the sense of touch.

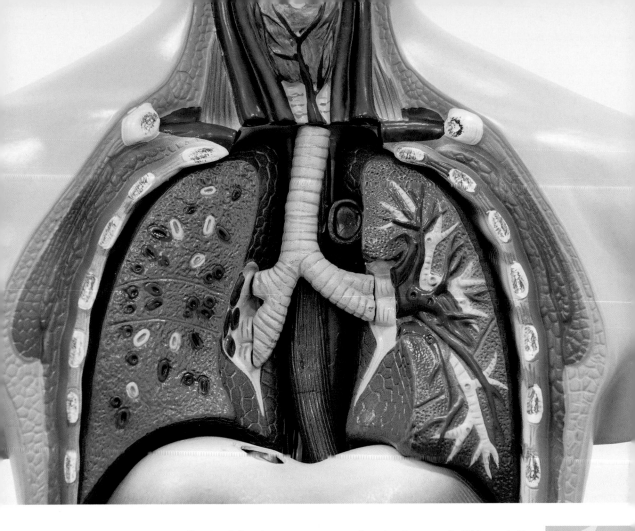

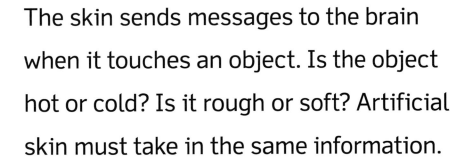
The trachea (light blue) is an important airway. Without it, humans would not be able to take in oxygen.

The skin sends messages to the brain when it touches an object. Is the object hot or cold? Is it rough or soft? Artificial skin must take in the same information.

Scientists have created artificial skin from plastic. It sends electrical signals to the brain. Some **prosthetic** hands are covered with artificial skin. These hands can sense whether a handshake is firm or weak.

LIKE THE REAL THING

Bioprinting is the process in which a 3D printer makes living tissue. 3D printers have been used to make artificial bones. They have printed artificial thyroid glands. They have made blood vessels and heart tissue. Soon they will be able to make other organs as well. Scientists revealed a 3D skin printer in 2018. The handheld printer releases a strip of skin tissue. Scientists hope the printer can be used to help burn victims.

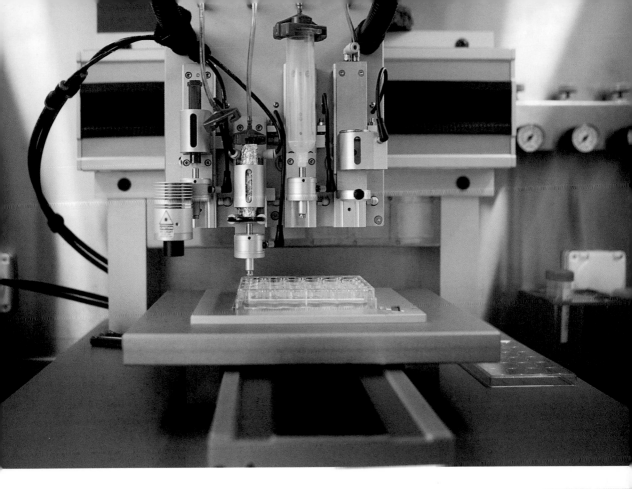

A bioprinter prints living tissue one layer at a time.

Thus far, artificial skin can sense only pressure. It cannot sense temperature or texture. Scientists are still working on improving artificial skin. They even hope to create skin that can heal itself.

CHAPTER 4

THE FUTURE OF ARTIFICIAL ORGANS

Scientists are always working on new artificial organs. They are also improving existing ones. As technology advances, patients with artificial organs are living longer. In the future, patients may no longer need transplants from donors. Artificial organs might become permanent solutions.

Scientists hope this new artificial heart will take the place of heart transplants.

In some cases, whole artificial organs won't be necessary. Engineers will print and grow tissue in a lab. The tissue will replace the parts of organs that aren't working. This process will be easier and quicker than performing a full transplant. It will also be less risky.

AN END TO ANIMAL TESTING

Today's medications are tested on animals. Scientists see how the animals react. Then they give the drugs to humans. This testing takes time and money. Many people also think that it is cruel to the animals. Human-made organs may one day make animal testing unnecessary. Engineers are making organs for use in drug tests. Scientists could test the organs' responses to drugs instead of using animals.

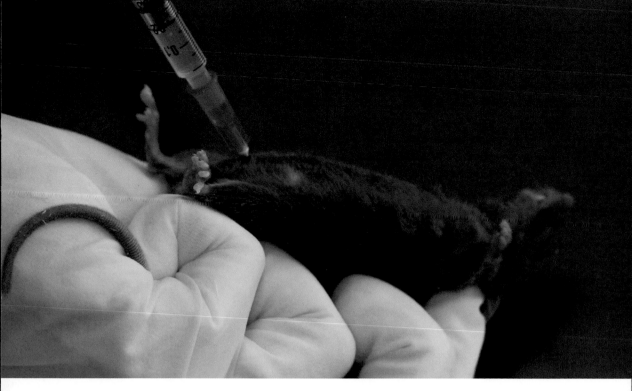

Researchers test experimental drugs on animals first. They make sure the drugs are safe for humans to use.

People with failing kidneys currently use dialysis machines. These machines perform the same work as kidneys. But they do not do the job as well. Scientists are designing an artificial kidney. It would be placed inside the body. It would remove toxins from the blood.

Scientists are also working on an artificial liver. Designing this organ is tricky. The liver does more than 500 jobs in the body. But its main job is helping with **metabolism**. Scientists are trying to grow livers from patients' own cells. They are also making machines that help failing livers work better. These devices could save the lives of patients waiting for transplants.

Computers could replace certain organs in the future. One example is the pancreas. This organ controls sugar levels in the body. Scientists are designing an artificial pancreas system. The device will not contain any artificial tissue. It will be

Researchers are testing an artificial pancreas that would monitor and respond to a patient's blood sugar levels.

a computer that works from inside the body. The computer will do the work of the pancreas.

Artificial organs have already saved lives. But they are still being improved. Future artificial organs will likely play an even greater role in saving patients' lives.

FOCUS ON
ARTIFICIAL ORGANS

Write your answers on a separate piece of paper.

1. Write a paragraph summarizing the main ideas from Chapter 1.

2. If you needed a new organ, would you be willing to receive an artificial one? Why or why not?

3. Which feeling can artificial skin currently sense?

    A. heat
    B. texture
    C. pressure

4. What job do artificial kidneys perform?

    A. They pump blood throughout the body.
    B. They remove toxins from the blood.
    C. They help control blood sugar.

Answer key on page 32.

GLOSSARY

arteries
Tubes through which blood flows from the heart to the rest of the body.

bionic
Made of artificial parts that enhance a natural capability.

dialysis
The process of removing waste from the blood.

donor
A person who provides tissue or an organ for transplant.

immune system
The body system that uses specialized cells to fight infections.

metabolism
The process of turning food and drink into energy for the body.

prosthetic
Having to do with artificial body parts.

stem cells
Cells that can divide and develop into more-specialized cells.

toxins
Poisonous substances.

TO LEARN MORE

BOOKS

Bethea, Nikole Brooks. *Discover Bionics*. Minneapolis: Lerner Publications, 2017.

Burillo-Kirch, Christine. *Bioengineering: Discover How Nature Inspires Human Designs with 25 Projects*. White River Junction, VT: Nomad Press, 2016.

Wood, John. *Medical Technology: Genomics, Growing Organs, and More*. New York: Gareth Stevens, 2018.

NOTE TO EDUCATORS

Visit **www.focusreaders.com** to find lesson plans, activities, links, and other resources related to this title.

INDEX

Answer Key: 1. Answers will vary; **2.** Answers will vary; **3.** C; **4.** B